J. Allen



# Scholastic Success With Addition & Subtraction

## Grade 2

by Danette Randolph

SCHOLASTIC
PROFESSIONAL BOOKS

New York • Toronto • London • Auckland • Sydney •
Mexico City • New Delhi • Hong Kong • Buenos Aires

Cover art by Amy Vangsgard
Cover design by Maria Lilja
Interior illustrations by Carol Tiernon
Interior design by Quack & Company

ISBN 0-439-44501-9



1 2 3 4 5 6 7 8 9 10 40 09 08 07 06 05 04 03

# Introduction

*Parents and teachers alike will find* **Addition & Subtraction** *to be a valuable learning tool. Children will enjoy completing a wide variety of math activities that are both engaging and educational. Take a look at the Table of Contents and you will feel rewarded providing such a valuable resource for your children.*

## Table of Contents

Name ____________________________________________ 

# Spell It Out

Add. Complete the puzzle using number words.

**Across**

1. 5 + 5 = ______
2. 3 + ______ = 7
3. 2 + ______ = 9
6. 6 + 2 = ______
7. ______ + 0 = 1

**Down**

1. 4 + ______ = 6
2. 2 + ______ = 7
3. ______ + 4 = 10
4. 4 + 5 = ______
5. 5 + ______ = 8

**Finish each number sentence with a number word.**

**five + two = ____________ three + six = ____________**

Name ______________________________________________

# Beautiful Bouquets

Subtract. Draw petals to show the difference.

**Color the bows with an even number yellow.**
**Color the bows with an odd number purple.**

# Crazy Creatures

Add or subtract. Fill in each missing number.

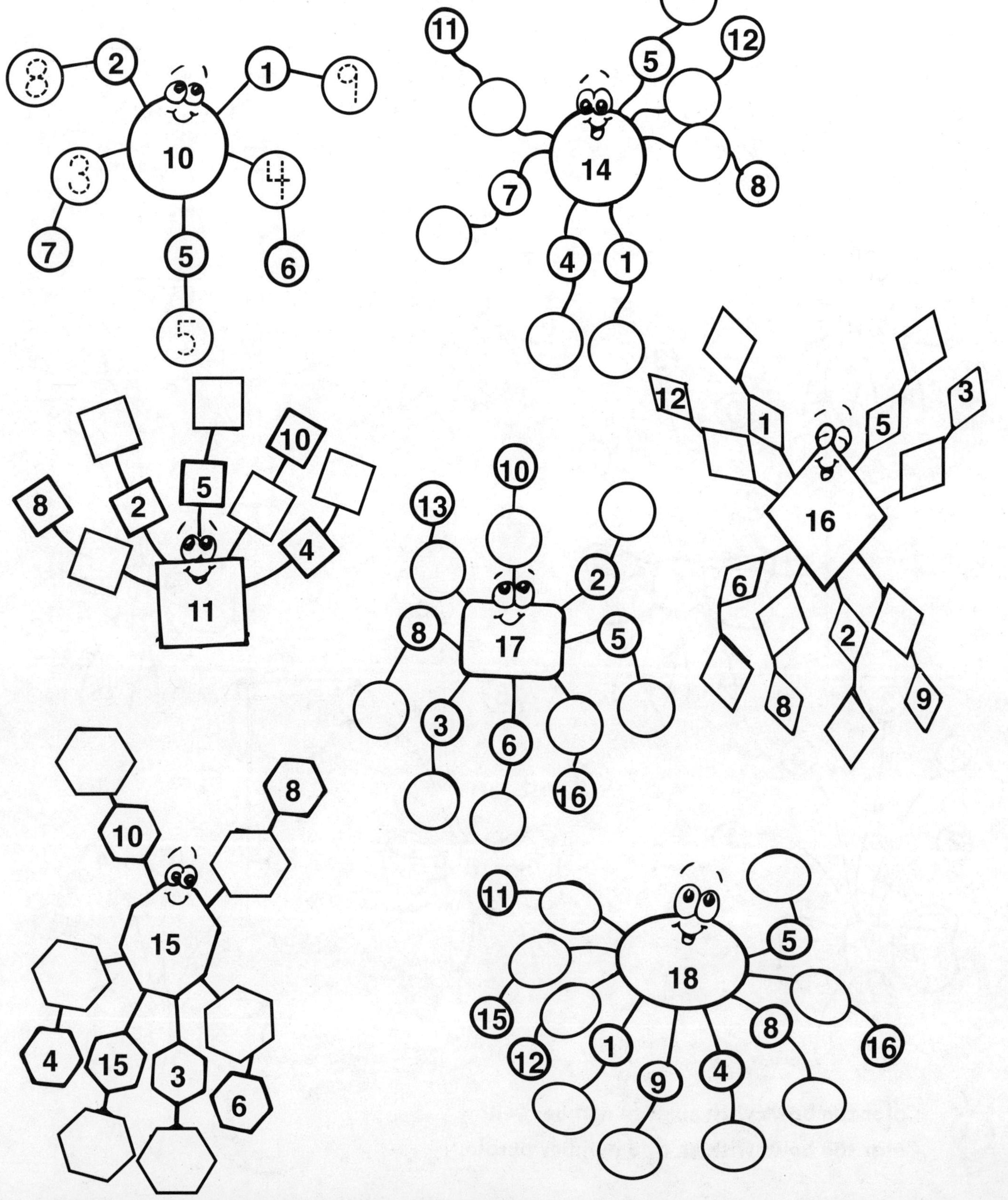

Name ______________________________



# Can You See It?

Write the numbers you see with a . . .

**A.**

sum of **5** and difference of **1**.

**B.**

sum of **17** and difference of **7**.

**C.**

sum of **14** and difference of **2**.

**D.**

sum of **18** and difference of **4**.

**E.**

sum of **12** and difference of **2**.

**F.**

sum of **15** and difference of **9**.

**G.**

sum of **5** and difference of **3**.

**H.**

sum of **18** and difference of **2**.

**I.**

sum of **13** and difference of **5**.

**J.**

sum of **16** and difference of **6**.

**Make your own number glasses.**

**sum of ________ and**

**difference of ______**

Name ______________________________________



# Counting on Good Manners

Add. Then use the code to write a letter in each oval to find the "good manner" words.

| | | | | | |
|---|---|---|---|---|---|
| 11<br>+ 10 | 62<br>+ 31 | 44<br>+ 34 | 41<br>+ 5 | 13<br>+ 31 | 35<br>+ 43 |
| | | | | | |

| | | | | |
|---|---|---|---|---|
| 40<br>+ 10 | 43<br>+ 24 | 42<br>+ 4 | 54<br>+ 25 | 41<br>+ 42 |
| | | | | |

| | | |
|---|---|---|
| 57<br>+ 2 | 22<br>+ 3 | 34<br>+ 32 |
| | | |

| | | | | |
|---|---|---|---|---|
| 54<br>+ 5 | 21<br>+ 4 | 41<br>+ 25 | 21<br>+ 11 | 26<br>+ 52 |
| | | | | |

| | | | | | | |
|---|---|---|---|---|---|---|
| 50<br>+ 30 | 70<br>+ 8 | 50<br>+ 43 | 11<br>+ 7 | 15<br>+ 10 | 31<br>+ 4 | 17<br>+ 61 |
| | | | | | | |

**Code**

| | | | | | | | |
|---|---|---|---|---|---|---|---|
| **18** C | **21** P | **25** O | **32** R | **35** M | **44** S | **46** A | **50** T |
| **59** Y | **66** U | **67** H | **78** E | **79** N | **80** W | **83** K | **93** L |

Name ______________________________

# Just the Same

Add. Connect the flowers with the same sum.

| | |
| --- | --- |
| $43 + 26$ | $52 + 36$ |
| $18 + 70$ | $23 + 22$ |
| $11 + 34$ | $51 + 18$ |
| $62 + 35$ | $14 + 11$ |
| $13 + 12$ | $55 + 42$ |

**Make matching sums.**

$\_\_ + \_\_ = 78$ $\_\_ + \_\_ = 78$

$\_\_ + \_\_ = 54$ $\_\_ + \_\_ = 54$

Name ______________________________



# Planet Earth

Add.

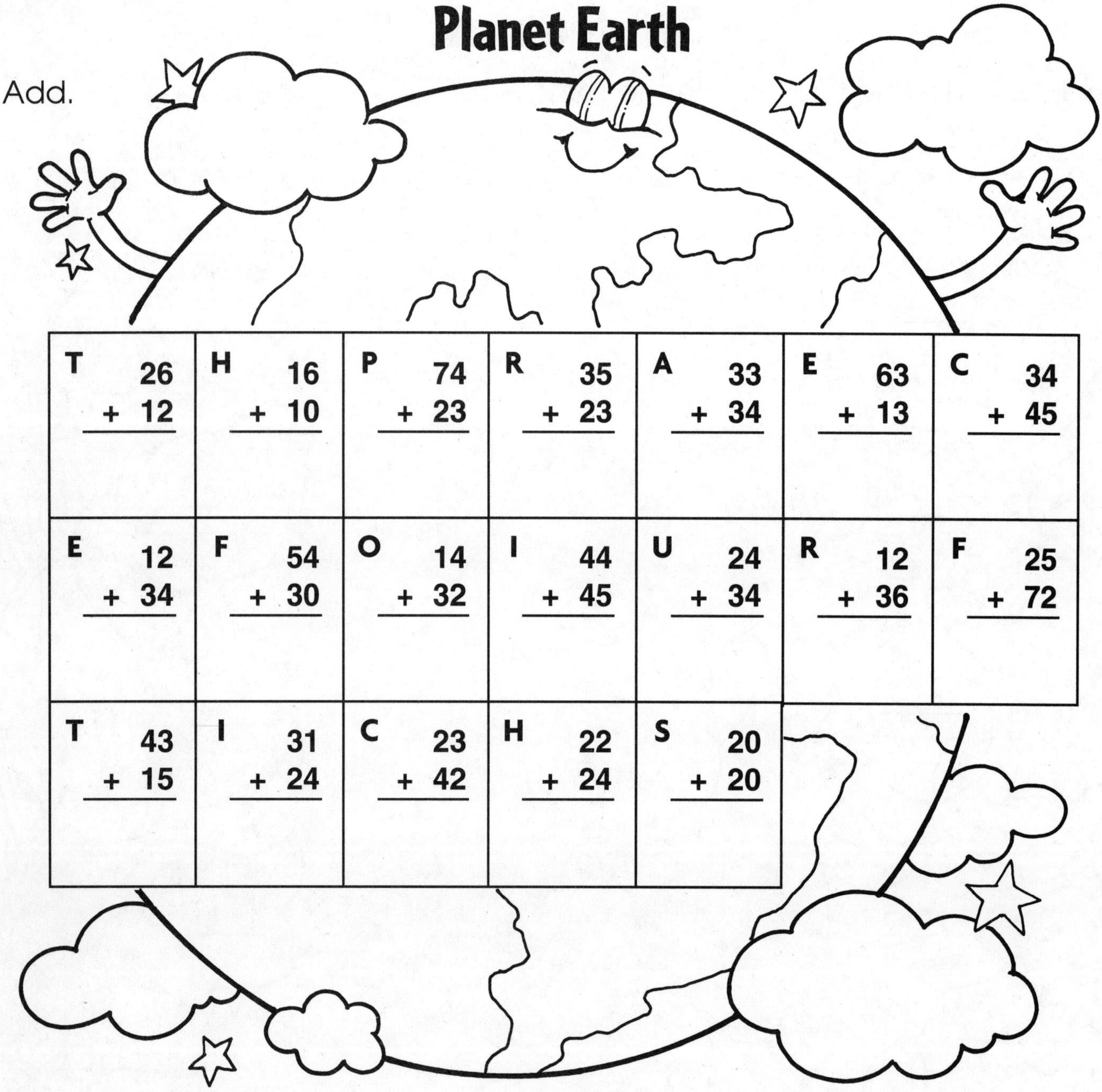

| | | | | | | |
|---|---|---|---|---|---|---|
| T 26 + 12 | H 16 + 10 | P 74 + 23 | R 35 + 23 | A 33 + 34 | E 63 + 13 | C 34 + 45 |
| E 12 + 34 | F 54 + 30 | O 14 + 32 | I 44 + 45 | U 24 + 34 | R 12 + 36 | F 25 + 72 |
| T 43 + 15 | I 31 + 24 | C 23 + 42 | H 22 + 24 | S 20 + 20 | | |

For each sum that is an even number, write its letter below in order.

**How much of the earth is covered by water?**

___ ___ ___ ___ ___ – ___ ___ ___ ___ ___ ___ ___

For each sum that is an odd number, write its letter below in order.

**What is the biggest ocean?**

___ ___ ___ ___ ___ ___ ___

Name ______________________



# High Flying

Subtract.

**Color the bird with the smallest number in the ones place red.**
**Color the bird with the smallest number in the tens place blue.**
**Color each bird with the same number in the ones and tens place green.**

Name ____________________



# Weather Drops

Subtract. Using the difference in each rain drop, write the weather words in order of their differences from least to greatest by the umbrella handle. Then color your favorite kind of "weather drop" blue.

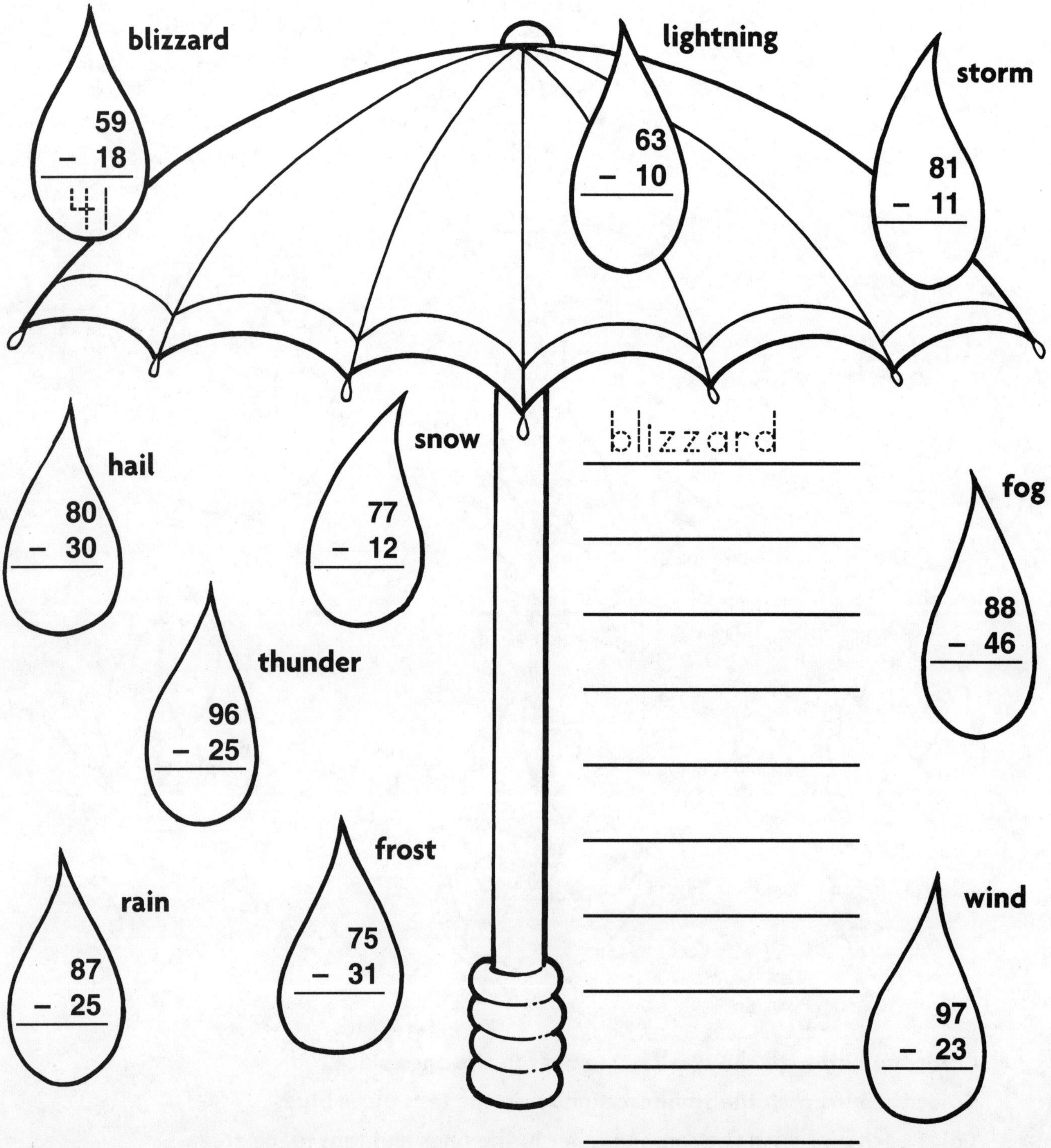

Name ____________________



# Animal Families

Subtract.

**Color the animals using the color code.**

| red | blue | purple | yellow | green |
|---|---|---|---|---|
| **32** | **43** | **54** | **67** | **85** |

# Triple the Fun

Add. Write the sum on each bowl.

**Color bowls with 1, 5, or 8 in the ones place yellow.**
**Color bowls with 0, 4, or 7 in the ones place pink.**
**Color bowls with 2, 6, or 9 in the ones place brown.**

Name ______________________________________



# A Great Catch

Circle each group of 10. Write the number of tens and ones on the chart. Then write the number on the baseball glove.

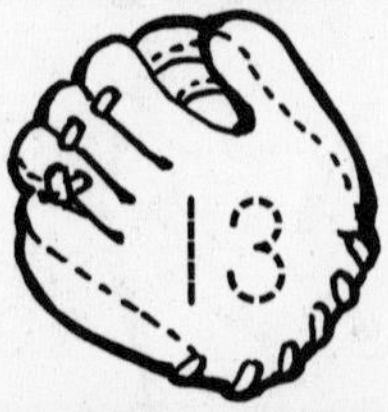


| tens | ones |
| --- | --- |
| 1 | 3 |

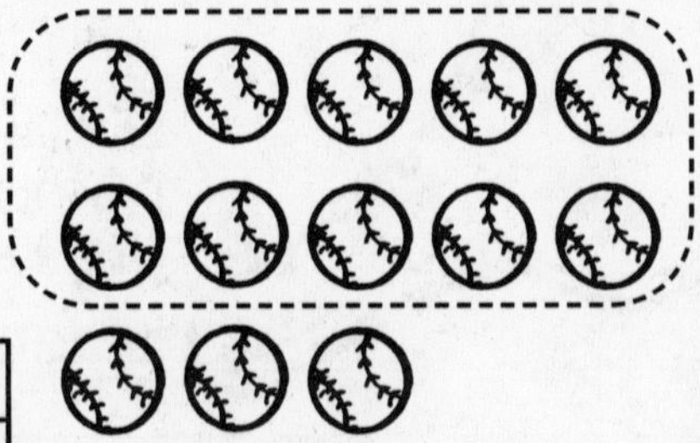

| tens | ones |
| --- | --- |
| | |

| tens | ones |
| --- | --- |
| | |

| tens | ones |
| --- | --- |
| | |

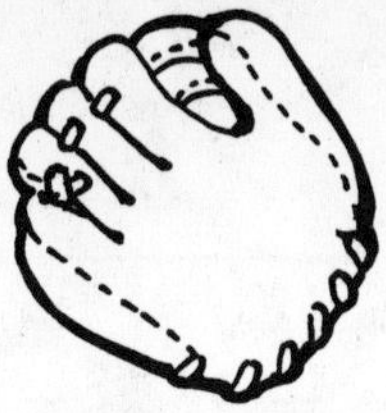

| tens | ones |
| --- | --- |
| | |

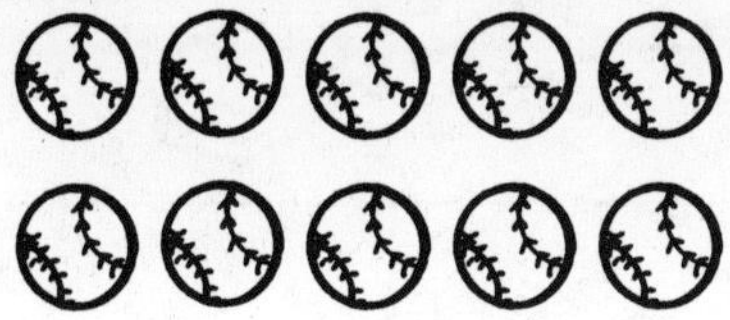

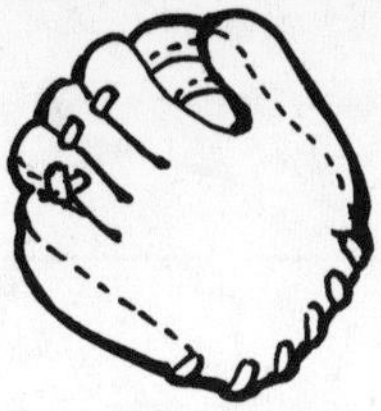

| tens | ones |
| --- | --- |
| | |

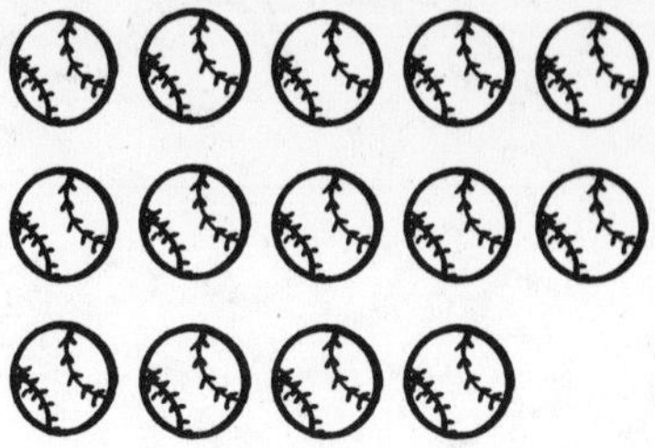

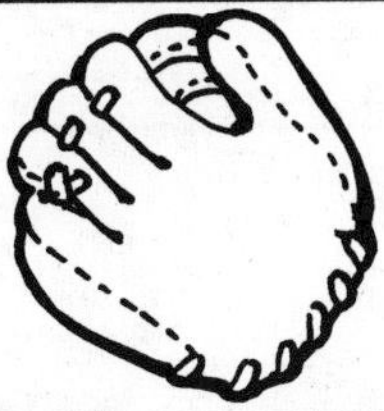

| tens | ones |
| --- | --- |
| | |

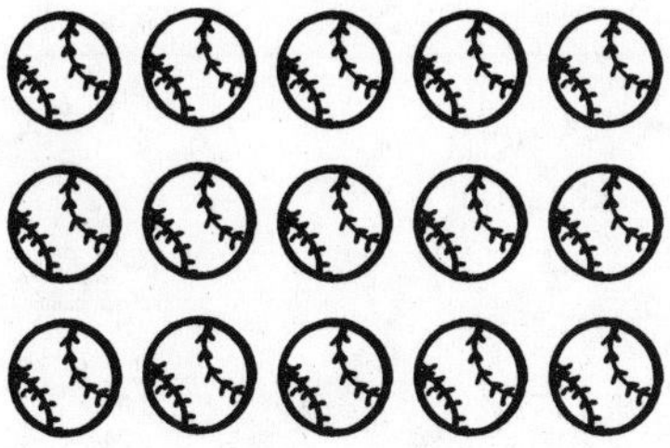

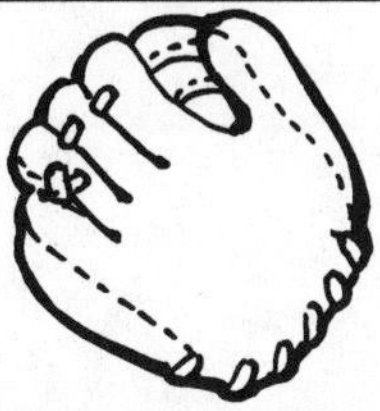

| tens | ones |
| --- | --- |
| | |

# Don't Forget Your Keys

Add. Then follow the clue to find the right key. Write the sum in the key hole.

**A.**

Find the key with the greatest number in the tens place.

**B.**

Find the key with the greatest number in the ones place.

**C.**

Find the key with even numbers in the ones and tens places.

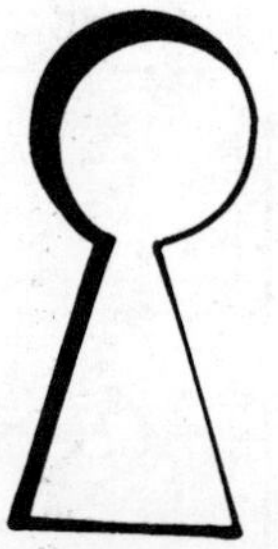

**D.**

Find the key with 0 in the ones place.

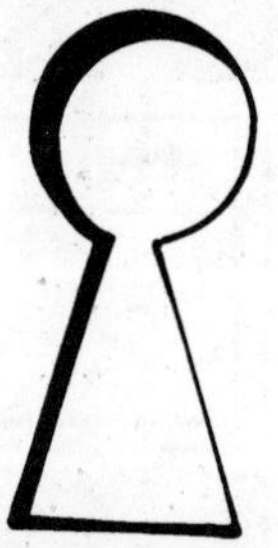

**E.**

Find the key with the same number in the ones and tens places.

# Treasure of a Book

Add. Then color each box with an odd sum to help the boy find his way to the book. Hint: Remember to look in the ones place.

| | | | | |
|---|---|---|---|---|
| | 47 + 24 | 74 + 19 | 78 + 12 | 15 + 37 |
| 48 + 44 | 31 + 59 | 52 + 39 | 29 + 57 | 73 + 19 |
| 63 + 18 | 14 + 67 | 57 + 16 | 24 + 18 | 63 + 29 |
| 57 + 28 | 27 + 47 | 76 + 16 | 72 + 18 | 76 + 18 |
| 32 + 19 | 17 + 24 | 55 + 38 | 32 + 49 | |

Name ______________________________



# How Do We Get There?

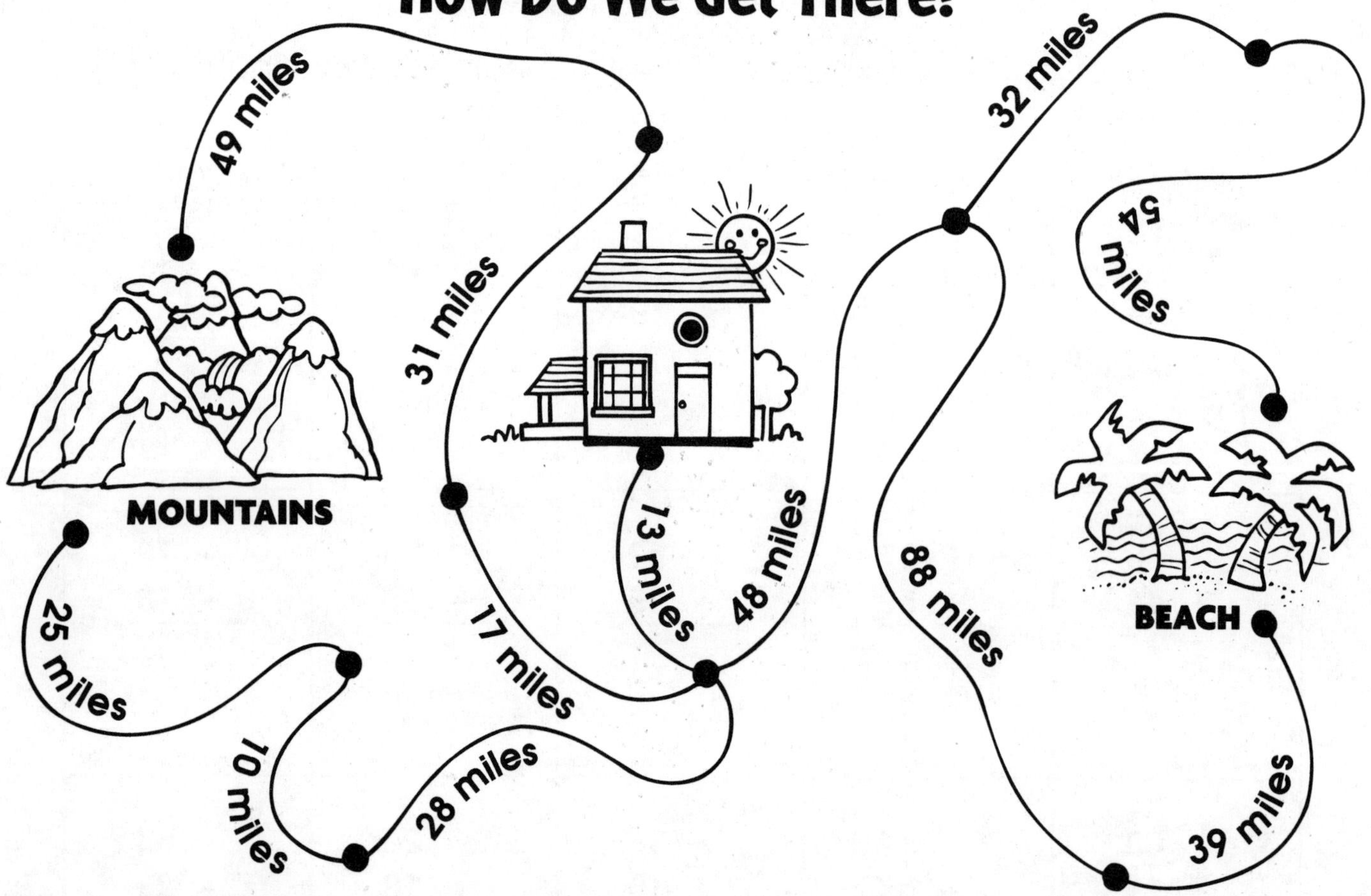


Add the distance of each route from the house to the beach.

| Route #1 | Route #2 |
| --- | --- |
| ____ | ____ |
| ____ | ____ |
| ____ | ____ |
| + ____ | + ____ |
| ________ miles | ________ miles |

Add the distance of each route from the house to the mountains.

| Route #1 | Route #2 |
| --- | --- |
| ____ | ____ |
| ____ | ____ |
| ____ | ____ |
| + ____ | + ____ |
| ________ miles | ________ miles |

Name ____________________



# Crack the Numbers

Look at the number on each chick. Write the number of tens and ones on the egg. Then trade one ten for ten ones.

2 tens
15 ones

_____ tens
_____ ones

_____ tens
_____ ones

_____ tens
_____ ones

_____ tens
_____ ones

_____ tens
_____ ones

Name ______________________________



# Digging Up Bones

Help Daisy find a delicious bone! Subtract.
Circle the answer that goes with each bone.

> is greater than and < is less than

**A.** > 40 and < 70

56 − 8 =

94 − 5 =

**B.** > 25 and < 55

87 − 8 =

53 − 7 =

**C.** > 37 and < 82

45 − 9 =

81 − 5 =

**D.** > 74 and < 96

83 − 6 =

68 − 9 =

**E.** > 18 and < 49

57 − 9 =

23 − 9 =

**F.** > 63 and < 87

70 − 9 =

75 − 7 =

**G.** > 16 and < 56

23 − 9 =

47 − 8 =

**Write two subtraction problems on another piece of paper. One answer should match the bone.**

> 48 and < 87

Name ______________________________



# First, Next, Last

Subtract. Then number the pictures in order from least to greatest.

**A.**

| | | |
|---|---|---|
| 64 | 58 | 83 |
| − 45 | − 19 | − 46 |

**B.**

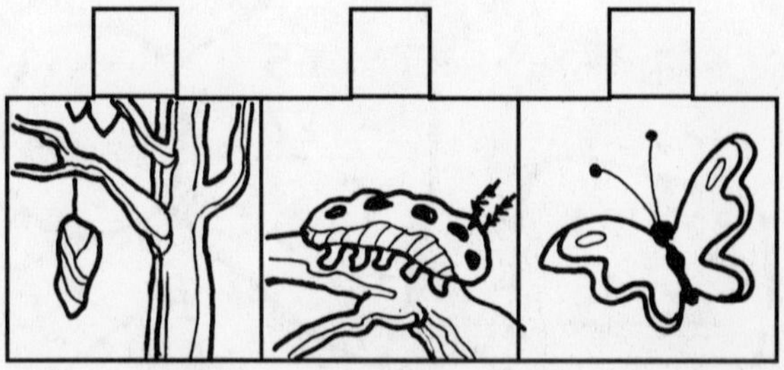

| | | |
|---|---|---|
| 83 | 24 | 28 |
| − 75 | − 18 | − 19 |

**C.**

| | | |
|---|---|---|
| 53 | 54 | 51 |
| − 25 | − 17 | − 37 |

**D.**

| | | |
|---|---|---|
| 88 | 91 | 82 |
| − 59 | − 53 | − 45 |

**E.**

| | | |
|---|---|---|
| 73 | 71 | 76 |
| − 44 | − 35 | − 28 |

**F.**

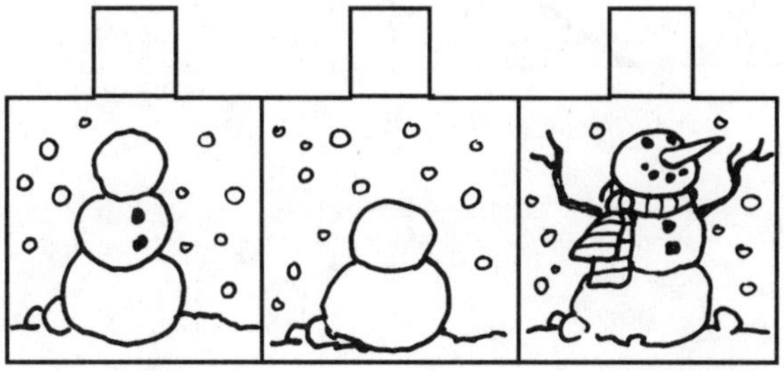

| | | |
|---|---|---|
| 82 | 34 | 57 |
| − 64 | − 19 | − 38 |

# All Tied Up

Subtract. Add to check.

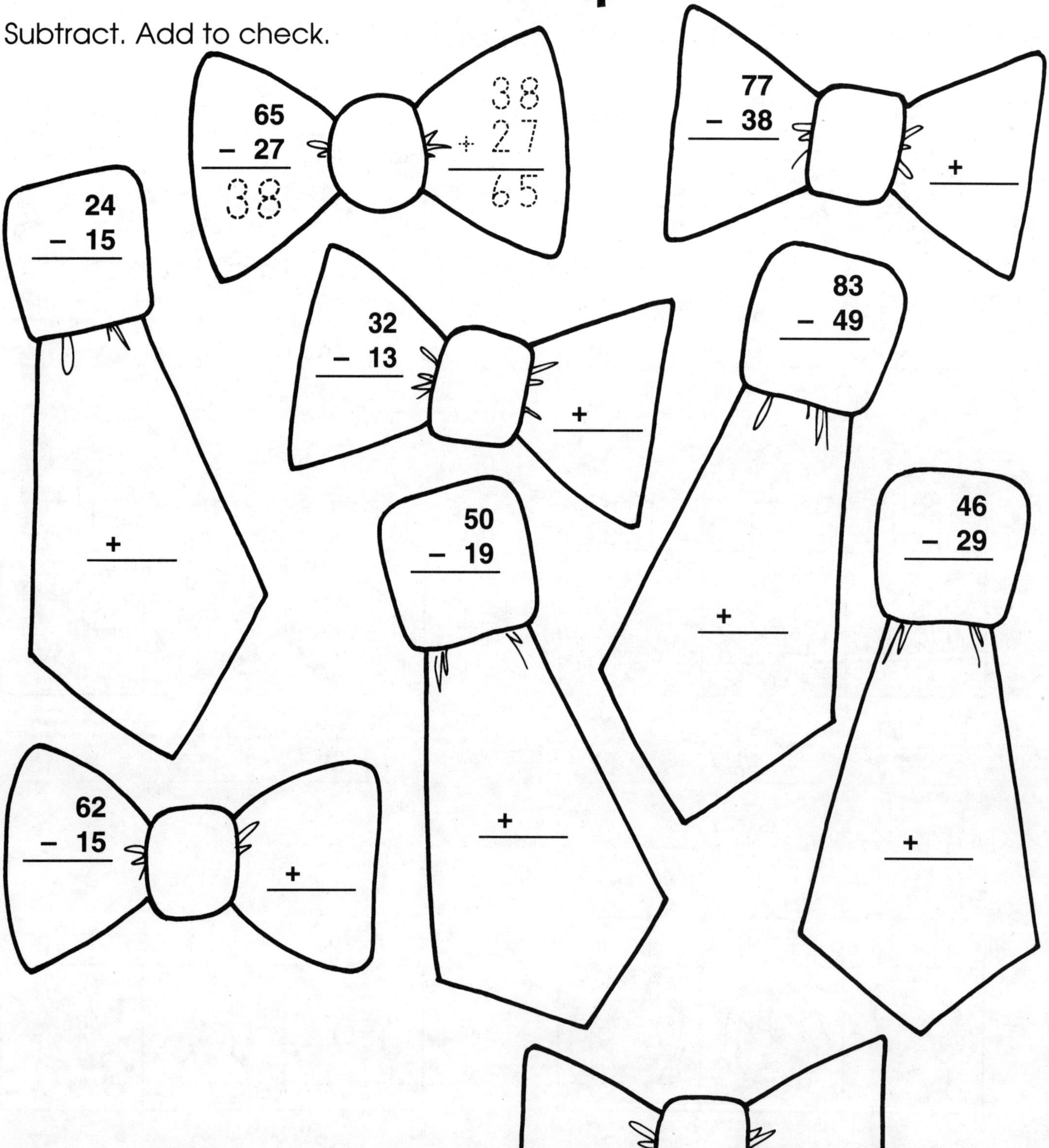


**Write your own subtraction problem. Add to check.**

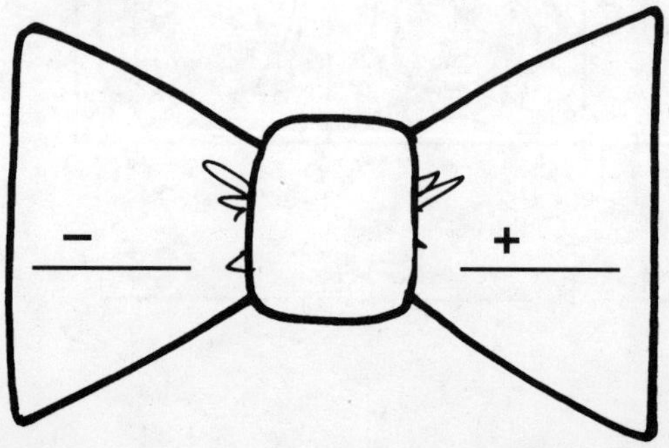

Name ______________________

# Teenie Tiny Babies

Add or subtract.

**U.** 42 + 39 = ____

**L.** 53 − 48 = ____

**N.** 31 + 29 = ____

**C.** 74 − 28 = ____

**O.** 44 + 46 = ____

**P.** 75 − 37 = ____

**H.** 40 − 17 = ____

**K.** 27 + 36 = ____

**S.** 96 − 48 = ____

**A.** 62 − 48 = ____

**G.** 80 − 62 = ____

**M.** 55 + 16 = ____

**R.** 88 − 19 = ____

Write the letter that goes with each number.

I am smaller than your thumb when I'm born.
___ ___ ___ ___ ___ ___ ___ ___
63 14 60 18 14 69 90 90

I am even smaller.
___ ___ ___ ___ ___
63 90 14 5 14

I am smaller than a bumblebee.
___ ___ ___ ___ ___ ___ ___
90 38 90 48 48 81 71

Since we are so little, we live right next to our mothers in a safe, warm ___ ___ ___ ___ ___.
38 90 81 46 23

Name ______________________________

Adding/subtracting 2-digit numbers with regrouping

# Day by Day

Add or subtract. Color each special date on the calendar.

## July

| Sun. | Mon. | Tues. | Wed. | Thur. | Fri. | Sat. |
|---|---|---|---|---|---|---|
| | | 1 | 2 | 3 | 4 | 5 |
| 6 | 7 | 8 | 9 | 10 | 11 | 12 |
| 13 | 14 | 15 | 16 | 17 | 18 | 19 |
| 20 | 21 | 22 | 23 | 24 | 25 | 26 |
| 27 | 28 | 29 | 30 | 31 | | |

**A.** Camp begins one week after the second Monday. Color this date red.

**B.** The baseball game is two weeks before the fourth Wednesday. Color this date green.

**C.** The birthday party is two weeks after the second Saturday. Color this date purple.

**D.** The swim meet is three weeks before the fifth Tuesday. Color this date blue.

**E.** The trip to the zoo is one week before the third Sunday. Color this date orange.

**F.** The picnic is two weeks before the fifth Thursday. Color this date yellow.

**G.** What date is 14 days after the third Wednesday? Color this date pink.

**H.** What date is 18 days before the fourth Friday? Color this date brown.

Name ______________________________

# Pizza Vote

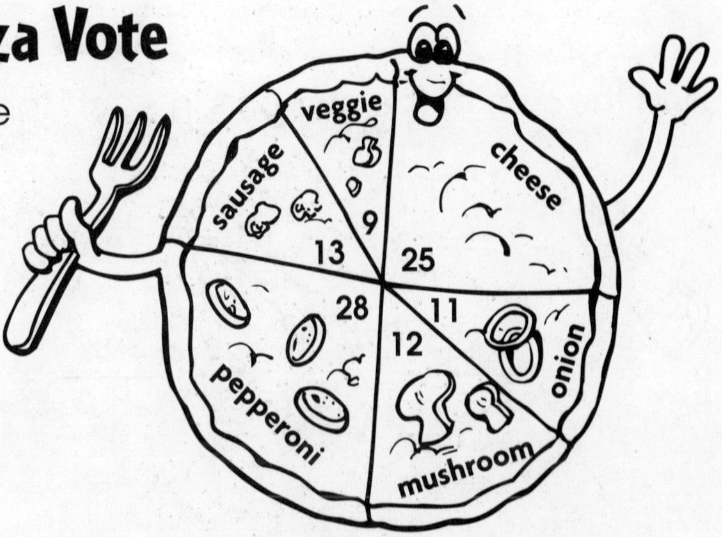


Use the circle graph to compare the results of the pizza vote.

**A.** How many students voted for pepperoni and cheese in all?

**B.** How many more students voted for cheese than veggie?

**C.** How many more students voted for pepperoni than sausage?

**D.** How many students voted for mushroom and veggie altogether?

**E.** How many more students voted for mushroom than veggie?

**F.** How many students voted for sausage and pepperoni in all?

**G.** How many students voted for veggie, cheese, and mushroom in all?

**Find the total number of students who voted.**

Name ______________________________



# Tool Time

Find the sum of the numbers in each tool.

34
27
+ 5
_____

+
_____

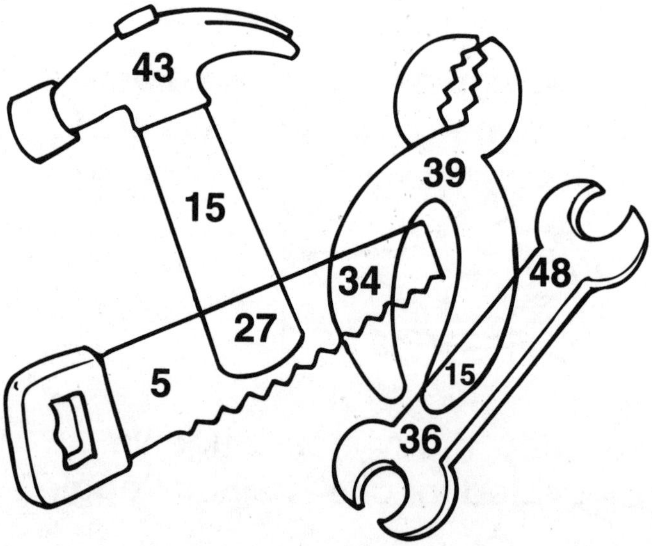

+
_____

+
_____

**A.** **Write the number found in the**  **and**  ☐

**Write the number found in the**  **and** **.** + ☐
_____

**Find the sum.**

**B.** **Find the difference between the largest and smallest numbers in each tool.**

 –
_____

 –
_____

 –
_____

 –
_____

**On another piece of paper, find the sum of the tools altogether.**
**Hint: You'll be adding nine numbers.**

Name ____________________



# Powerful Presidents

Add. Color each even sum red to learn about George Washington. Color each odd sum blue to learn about Abe Lincoln. Hint: Look in the ones place.

**A.** the "Father of the Country"

423
+ 173

**B.** born in 1809 in Kentucky

384
+ 611

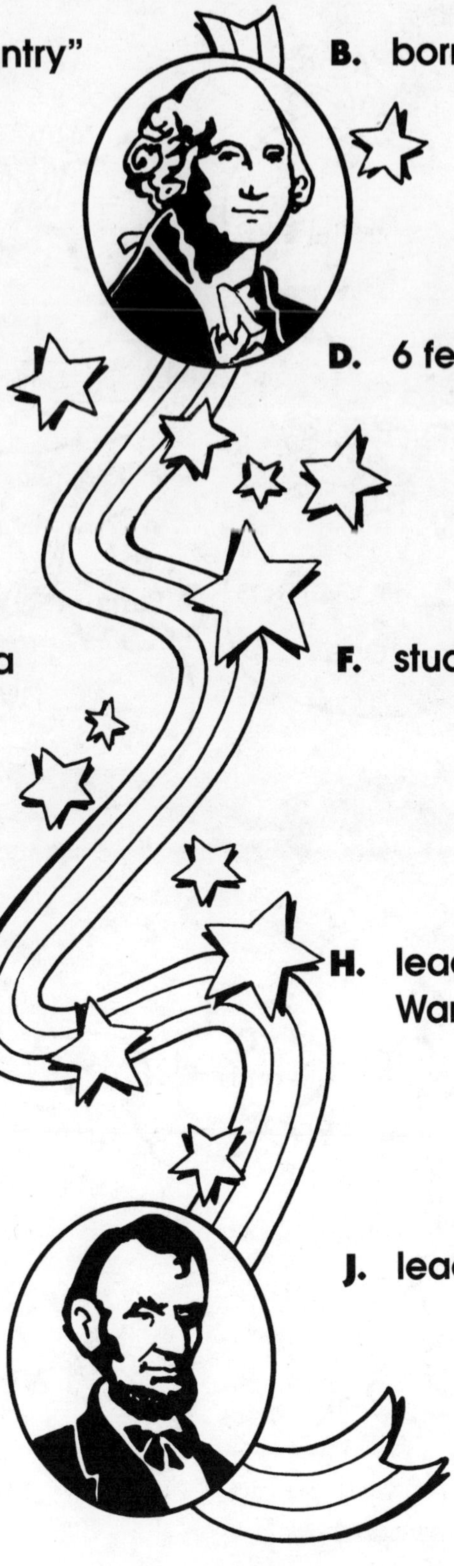

**C.** sixteenth president

325
+ 552

**D.** 6 feet 4 inches tall

257
+ 312

**E.** born in 1732 in Virginia

101
+ 561

**F.** studied geography

570
+ 408

**G.** first president

805
+ 163

**H.** leader in the Revolutionary War

445
+ 151

**I.** loved reading books

609
+ 290

**J.** leader in the Civil War

314
+ 183

Name ______________________________



# Hundreds of Pumpkins

Regroup tens into hundreds. Remember: 10 tens = 1 hundred. Write the number of hundreds and the number of remaining tens.

**27 tens**
__2__ hundreds
__7__ tens

**84 tens**
_____ hundreds
_____ tens

**93 tens**
_____ hundreds
_____ tens

**71 tens**
_____ hundreds
_____ tens

**56 tens**
_____ hundreds
_____ tens

**32 tens**
_____ hundreds
_____ tens

**49 tens**
_____ hundreds
_____ tens

**65 tens**
_____ hundreds
_____ tens

Write the number.

**5 hundreds** **7 tens** **0 ones**

**8 hundreds** **0 tens** **4 ones**

Name ______________________________________



# Through the Tunnels

Add. Then trace the mole's path to the top. The mole must travel through tunnels with a zero in the sum.

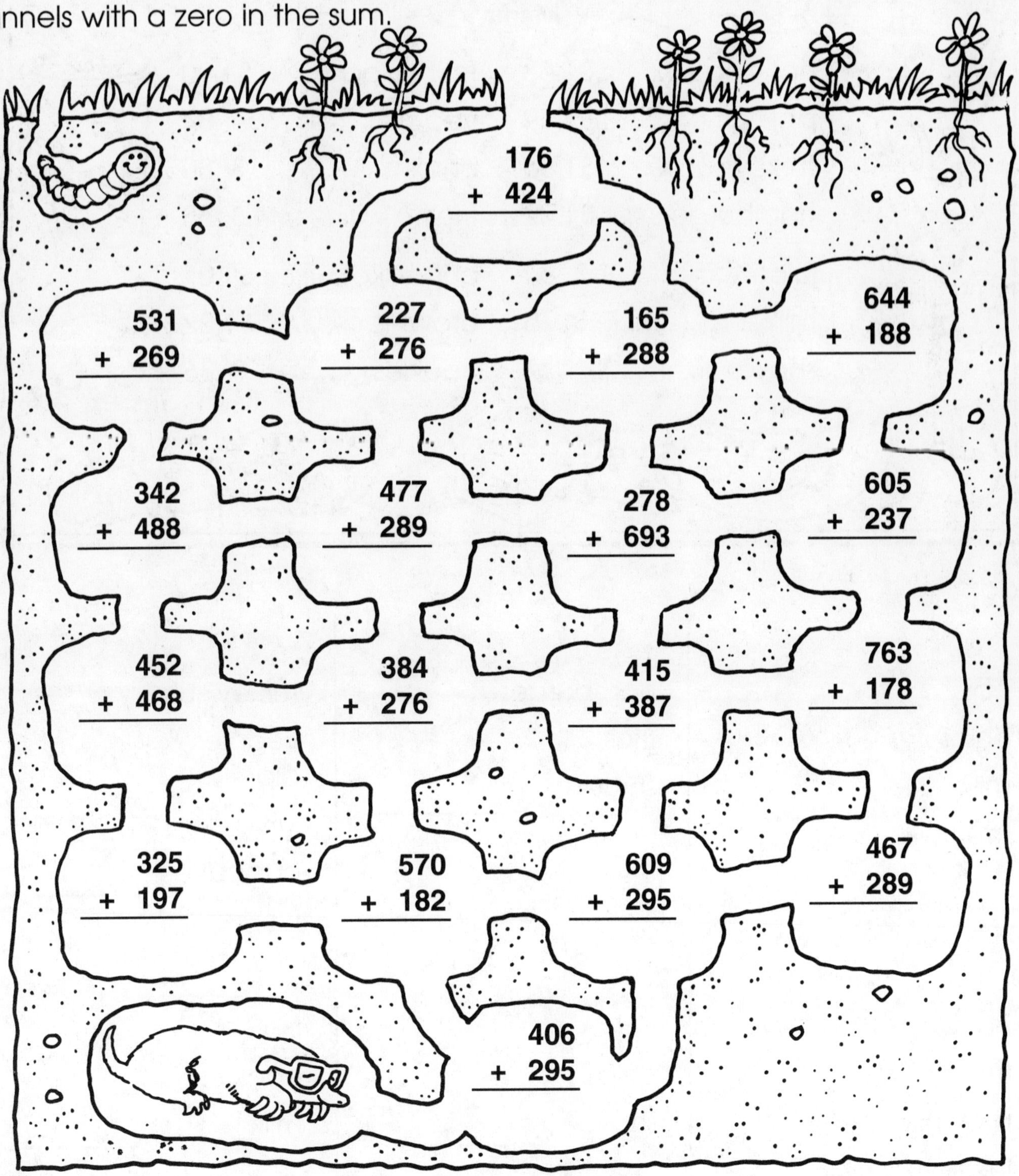


**On another piece of paper, write three more problems that have a zero in the sum.**

# Sandwich Shop

**Menu**

| | | | |
|---|---|---|---|
| hot dog | $1.53 | fruit salad | $1.90 |
| pbj | $1.49 | veggies & dip | $1.84 |
| turkey sub | $1.86 | chips | $ .50 |
| hamburger | $1.72 | fries | $ .65 |
| juice | $ .84 | cupcake | $1.07 |
| milk | $ .75 | brownie | $1.22 |
| shake | $1.17 | cookies | $ .86 |

Add.

**A.**

pbj
chips
milk
brownie +

**B.**

hamburger
fries
shake +

**C.**

turkey sub
veggies & dip
juice
cupcake +

**D.**

hot dog
fruit salad
brownie
juice +

**E.**

turkey sub
chips
shake +

**F.**

pbj
cookies
milk +

Name ______________________________



# Easy as 1, 2, 3

Add to find the perimeter of each shape.

**A.**

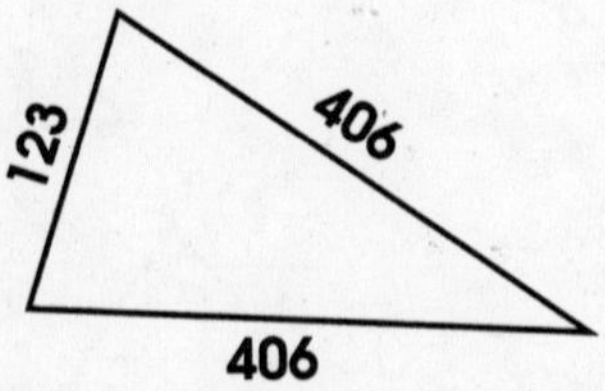


**B.**

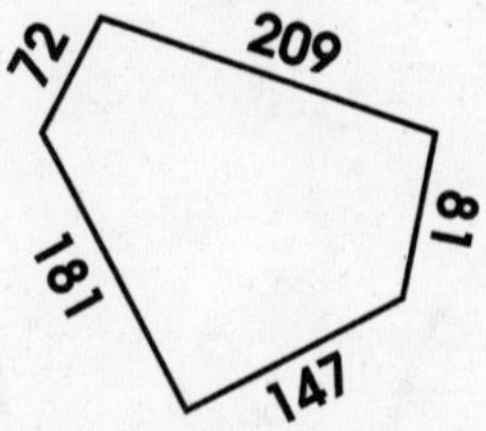


**C.**

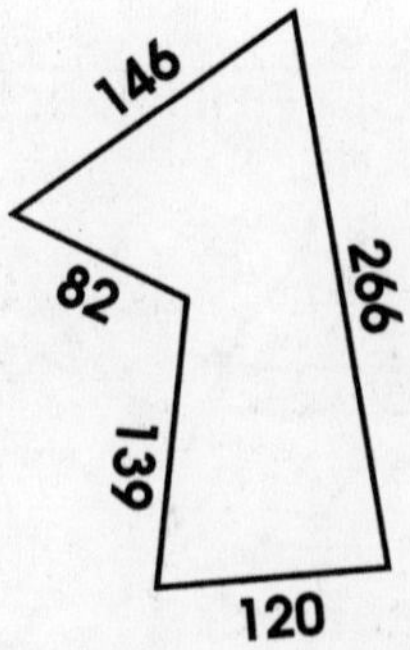


```
   123
   406
 + 406
 ─────
```

+ ______

+ ______

**D.**

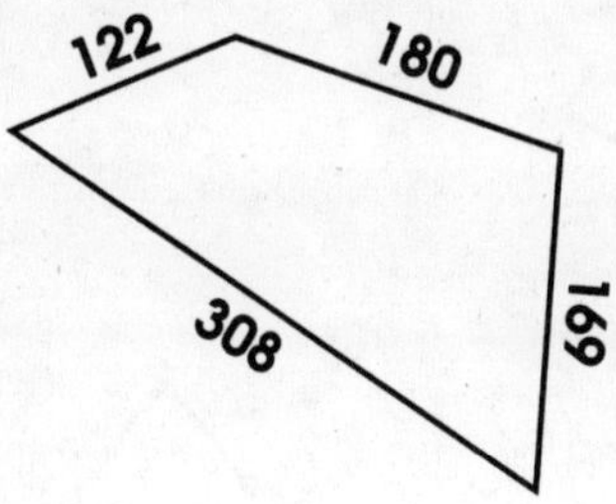


**E.**

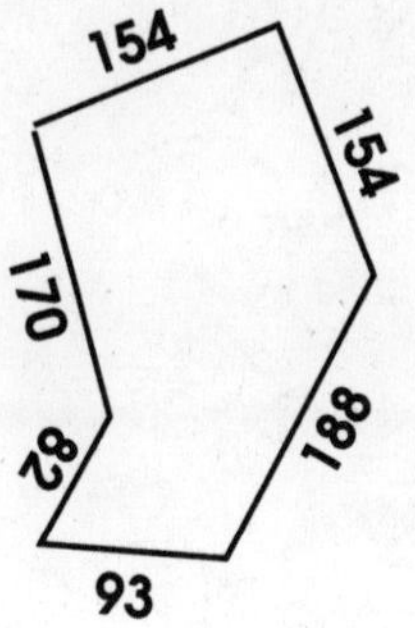


**F.**

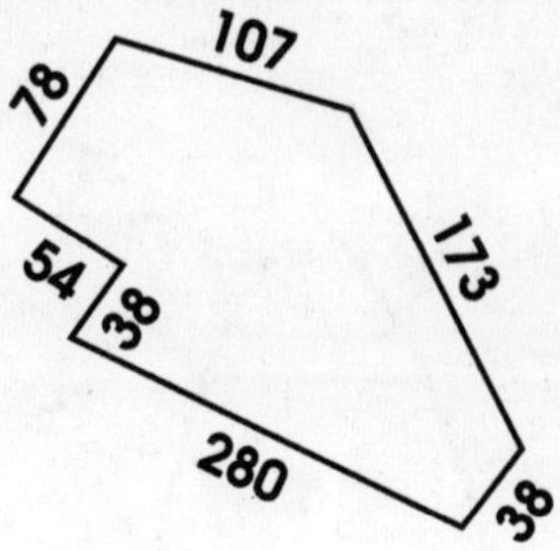


+ ______

+ ______

+ ______

**Color each shape using the code below.**

| | | |
|---|---|---|
| **9 hundreds — orange** | **4 tens — red** | **3 ones — purple** |
| **6 hundreds — green** | **7 tens — yellow** | **8 ones — blue** |

Name ______________________



# Count Down

Regroup hundreds to tens. Remember: 1 hundred = 10 tens.

Name ______________________________



# The Sun's Family

Draw a line to each matching difference to connect each planet to a fact about it.

| | |
|---|---|
| **Mars**  | 694 − 421 |
| **Saturn**  | 935 − 123 |
| **Mercury**  | 573 − 241 |
| **Pluto**  | 937 − 304 |
| **Earth**  | 437 − 225 |
| **Uranus**  | 968 − 413 |

| | |
|---|---|
| 397 − 185 | I am a ball of rock and metal but covered with soil, rock, and water. |
| 982 − 650 | I am a bare, rocky ball similar to Earth's moon. |
| 847 − 214 | I am usually the farthest planet from the sun. |
| 963 − 151 | I am surrounded by seven flat rings made of pieces of ice. |
| 857 − 302 | I am a planet with 15 moons. |
| 596 − 323 | I am called the Red Planet. |

# A Place in Space

Draw a line to each matching difference to connect each planet or space object to a fact about it.

**Venus**

$$\begin{array}{r} 713 \\ -\ 171 \\ \hline \end{array}$$

**Neptune**

$$\begin{array}{r} 833 \\ -\ 117 \\ \hline \end{array}$$

**Jupiter**

$$\begin{array}{r} 675 \\ -\ 216 \\ \hline \end{array}$$

**Moon**

$$\begin{array}{r} 407 \\ -\ 223 \\ \hline \end{array}$$

**Comet**

$$\begin{array}{r} 514 \\ -\ 126 \\ \hline \end{array}$$

---

$$\begin{array}{r} 952 \\ -\ 236 \\ \hline \end{array}$$

I am a planet with days lasting only 16 hours.

$$\begin{array}{r} 857 \\ -\ 469 \\ \hline \end{array}$$

I am like a dirty snowball made of dust, ice, and gases.

$$\begin{array}{r} 612 \\ -\ 428 \\ \hline \end{array}$$

I am covered with craters.

$$\begin{array}{r} 931 \\ -\ 389 \\ \hline \end{array}$$

I am sizzling hot with no water.

$$\begin{array}{r} 892 \\ -\ 433 \\ \hline \end{array}$$

I am a giant planet with a red spot.

**Complete each pattern. Then tell someone the pattern for each set of numbers.**

**900, 800, 700, ______, ______, ______, ______, ______, ______**

**900, 700, 500, ______, ______**

**800, 600, 400, ______**

# Tricky Zero

Subtract.

```
  480      360      190      720
- 136    - 318    - 124    - 517
-----    -----    -----    -----

  208      904      502      500
- 129    - 435    - 289    - 247
-----    -----    -----    -----

  800      305      490      300
- 643    - 176    - 256    - 134
-----    -----    -----    -----

                    700
                  - 391
                  -----
```

Name ____________________



# Treasures Under the Sea

Add or subtract. Use the chart to color the picture.

| | |
|---|---|
| 53 | white |
| 187 | pink |
| 264 | brown |
| 319 | purple |
| 420 | green |
| 837 | blue |
| 900 | yellow |

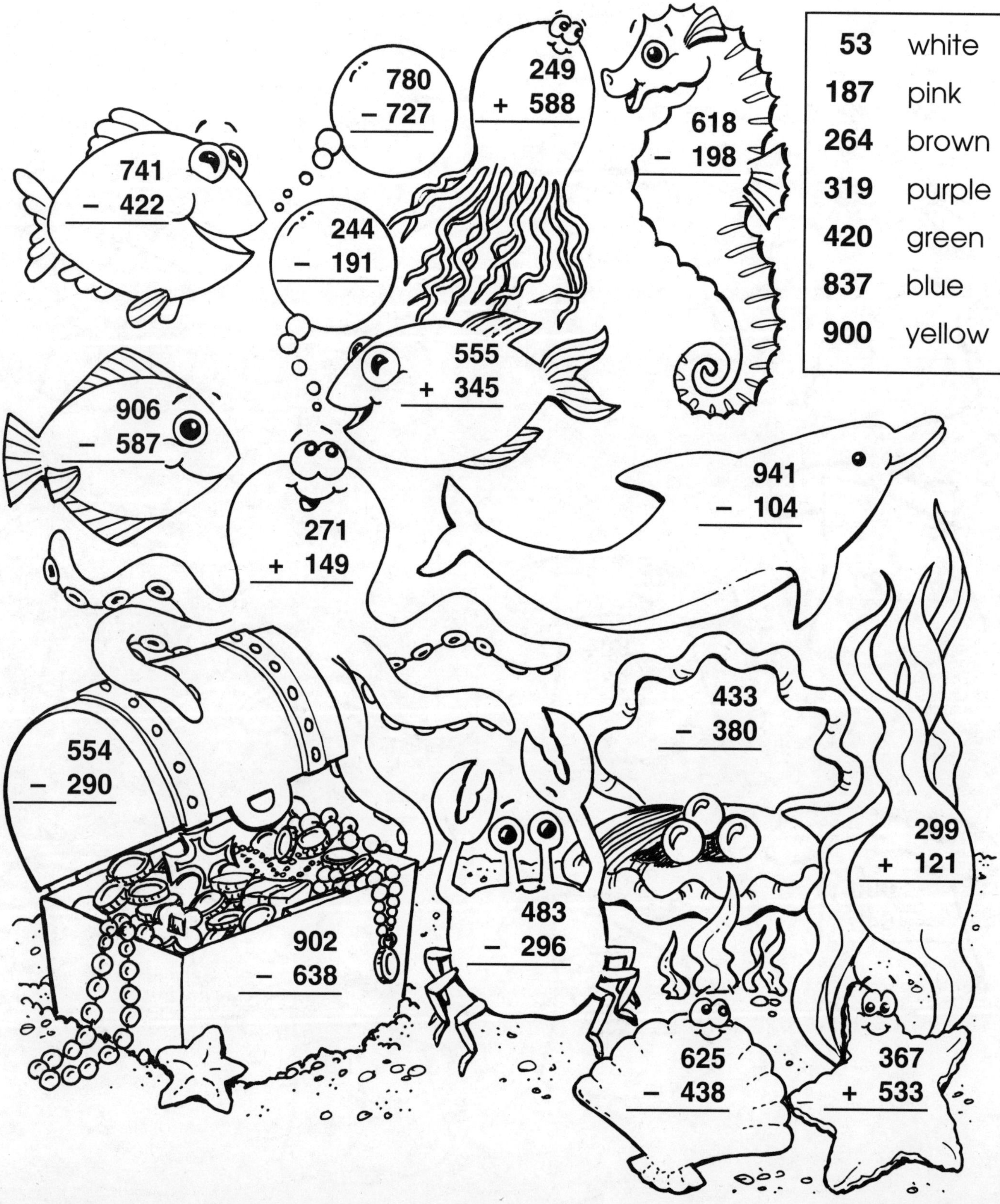

Name ______________________________ **Adding/subtracting 3-digit numbers with regrouping**

# Follow the Trees

Add or subtract. Then trace the bear's path to its cave. The bear follows trees with sums that have a 3 in the tens place.

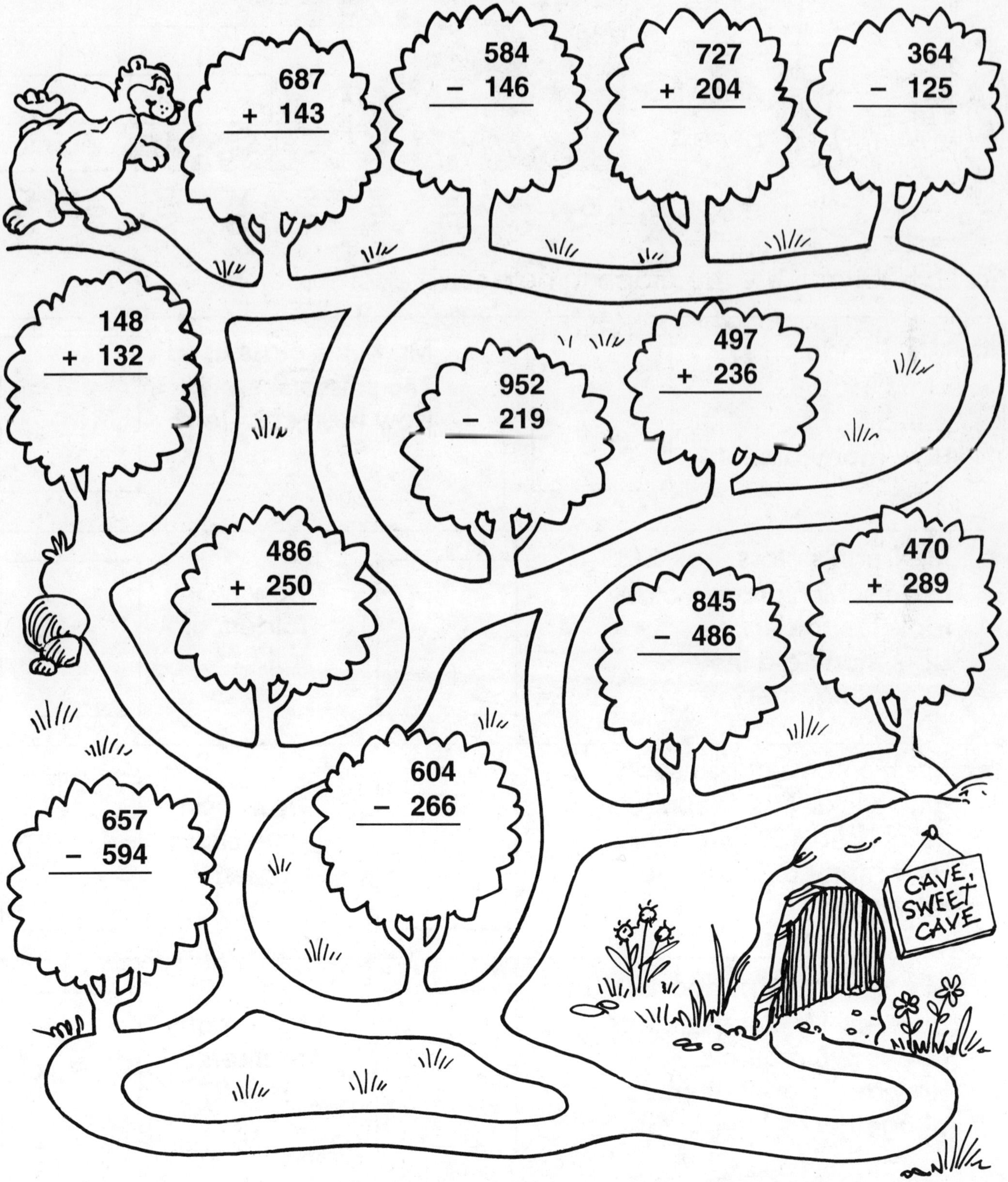

Name ____________________________________________



# School Supplies

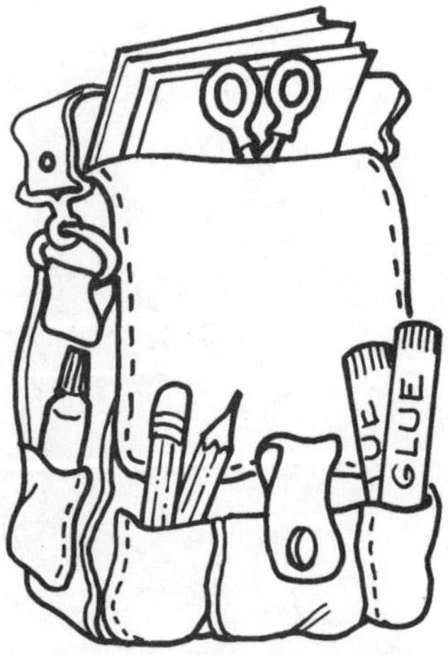


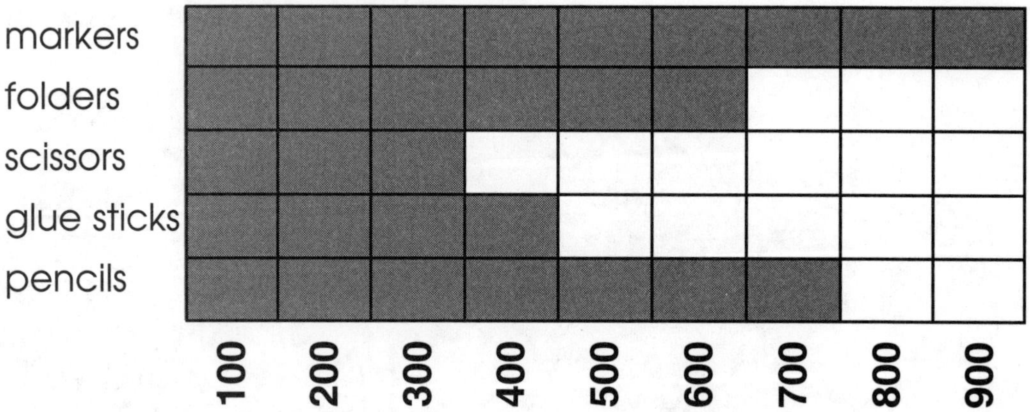


Add or subtract. Use the graph to help solve each problem.

**A.** Mrs. Randolph's class used 523 pencils.
How many are left? ☐

**B.** Mr. Kirk's class used 156 scissors.
How many are left? ☐

**C.** Mr. Dean's class took 248 folders. Mr. Jordan's class took 176 folders.
How many did they take altogether? ☐

How many folders are left? ☐

**D.** Mrs. Fenton's class used 96 glue sticks. Mrs. McBride's class used 189 glue sticks.
How many did they use altogether? ☐

How many glue sticks are left? ☐

**E.** Mrs. Barry's class needs 275 markers. Mr. Lopez's class needs 398 markers.
How many do they need altogether? ☐

How many markers are left? ☐

# Movie Madness

Add or subtract to solve.

**A.** 168 people are in line to buy tickets. 159 seats are available in the theater. How many people will not get a ticket to the movie?

**B.** 427 people attended the rush hour show. 289 people attended the 7:00 show. How many attended both shows altogether?

**C.** 507 people ordered a popcorn and a soda. 278 people ordered popcorn only. How many more people ordered a soda?

**D.** 319 people bought a pretzel. 299 people bought a box of candy. How many pretzels and candy were sold altogether?

**E.** There were 826 people at the movie theater on Friday. On Saturday, there were 697 people. How many more people were at the movie theater on Friday?

**F.** 258 people ordered a hot dog with mustard. 273 people ordered a hot dog with ketchup. How many hot dogs were ordered in all?

Name ____________________

**Adding/subtracting 3-digit numbers with regrouping**

# Animal Facts

Add or subtract.

| | | | | | | |
|---|---|---|---|---|---|---|
| **T** 247 + 253 | **O** 463 + 440 | **L** 217 + 68 | **P** 639 + 207 | **A** 391 + 144 | **W** 459 + 492 | **I** 198 + 672 |
| **P** 842 − 314 | **L** 504 + 475 | **I** 500 − 293 | **R** 457 + 364 | **I** 903 − 339 | **O** 107 + 147 | **A** 924 − 71 |
| **N** 700 − 427 | **N** 903 − 34 | **R** 703 − 186 | **H** 258 + 553 | **A** 357 + 537 | | |

Move across each row. Write the letter from each box with the correct number of hundreds.

| | | |
|---|---|---|
| **2 hundreds** | I am a cat that likes to sleep 20 hours a day. | ☐☐☐☐ |
| **5 hundreds** | I have four toes on my front feet and three toes on my back feet. | ☐☐☐☐☐ |
| **8 hundreds** | I am a fish with razor-sharp teeth. | ☐☐☐☐☐☐☐ |
| **9 hundreds** | I can see well at night but cannot move my eyes. | ☐☐☐ |

Name ______________________________

Adding/subtracting 3-digit numbers with regrouping

# Very Special Helpers

Add or subtract. Write the letter that goes with each answer in the center.

| B | E | L | H | F | D | A |
|---|---|---|---|---|---|---|
| 207 + 566 | 814 − 245 | 339 + 128 | 540 − 166 | 422 − 174 | 615 − 230 | 409 + 387 |

N: 772 − 484

I: 635 + 199

O: 596 + 287

M: 841 − 152

C: 600 − 341

T: 478 + 418

R: 603 + 197

P: 416 + 288

___ ___ ___ ___ ___ ___ ___
248 834 800 569 689 796 288

___ ___ ___ ___ ___ ___ ___
896 569 796 259 374 569 800

___ ___ ___ ___ ___ ___
385 883 259 896 883 800

___ ___ ___ ___ ___ ___ ___ ___ ___
467 834 773 800 796 800 834 796 288

___ ___ ___ ___ ___ ___ ___ ___ ___
704 883 467 834 259 569 689 796 288

Name ______________________________



# Vacation Time

Write the name and the price of each item in the correct suitcase. Add the prices.

$.77

$7.14

**Beach**

______________ $______

______________ $______

______________ $______

______________ $______

Total $

$2.10

$6.89

**Mountains**

______________ $______

______________ $______

______________ $______

______________ $______

Total $

$1.23

$1.23

$3.74

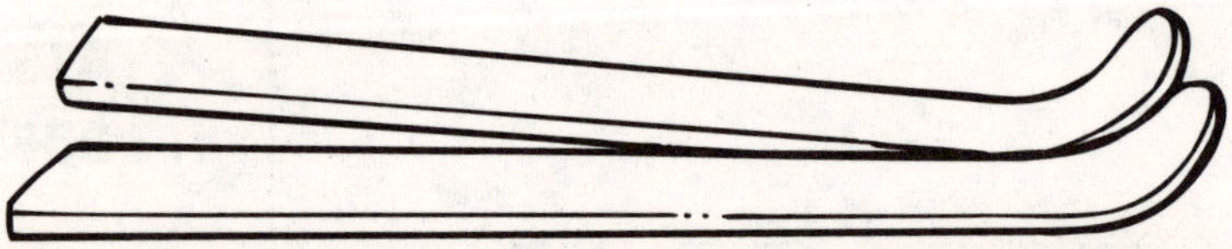

$1.46

**How much more does it cost to fill the mountain suitcase than the beach suitcase? Show your work on another piece of paper.**

Name ______________________________



# Bull's-eye

Select any problem. Add or subtract. Color the answer on the target. Repeat until you hit the bull's-eye. Then answer the remaining problems.

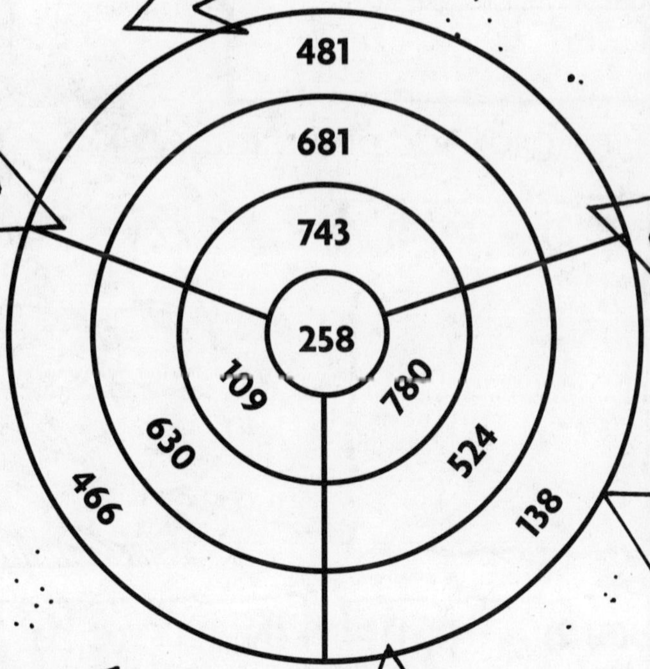


$$\begin{array}{r} 486 \\ +\ 294 \\ \hline \end{array}$$

$$\begin{array}{r} 653 \\ -\ 187 \\ \hline \end{array}$$

$$\begin{array}{r} 343 \\ +\ 287 \\ \hline \end{array}$$

$$\begin{array}{r} 800 \\ -\ 276 \\ \hline \end{array}$$

$$\begin{array}{r} 404 \\ -\ 146 \\ \hline \end{array}$$

$$\begin{array}{r} 628 \\ -\ 519 \\ \hline \end{array}$$

$$\begin{array}{r} 680 \\ -\ 199 \\ \hline \end{array}$$

$$\begin{array}{r} 974 \\ -\ 836 \\ \hline \end{array}$$

$$\begin{array}{r} 347 \\ +\ 396 \\ \hline \end{array}$$

$$\begin{array}{r} 505 \\ +\ 176 \\ \hline \end{array}$$

**Write how many "tries" it took for you to hit the bull's-eye.** ☐

# Grid Math

| | | | | |
|---|---|---|---|---|
| 3 | 550 | 636 | 282 | 963 |
| 2 | 189 | 148 | 579 | 415 |
| 1 | 427 | 751 | 370 | 804 |
| | A | B | C | D |

Find the numbers on the grid. Add or subtract.

(A, 1) + (C, 3)

(B, 3) − (A, 3)

(D, 3) − (A, 2)

(B, 2) + (C, 1)

(A, 3) + (C, 1)

(D, 1) − (B, 3)

(A, 2) + (B, 1)

(C, 2) − (C, 3)

(D, 3) − (B, 2)

(D, 2) + (A, 2)

Name ______________________________



# Perfect Punt

Add or subtract. Draw a line to connect each football to its goalpost.

$$\begin{array}{r} 423 \\ +\ 267 \\ \hline \end{array}$$

$$\begin{array}{r} 742 \\ -\ 543 \\ \hline \end{array}$$

$$\begin{array}{r} 903 \\ -\ 189 \\ \hline \end{array}$$

$$\begin{array}{r} 513 \\ -\ 276 \\ \hline \end{array}$$

$$\begin{array}{r} 409 \\ +\ 159 \\ \hline \end{array}$$

$$\begin{array}{r} 192 \\ +\ 285 \\ \hline \end{array}$$

$$\begin{array}{r} 604 \\ +\ 247 \\ \hline \end{array}$$

$$\begin{array}{r} 584 \\ +\ 317 \\ \hline \end{array}$$

$> 600$ and $< 700$

$> 200$ and $< 300$

$> 800$ and $< 900$

$> 100$ and $< 200$

$> 500$ and $< 600$

$> 700$ and $< 800$

$> 400$ and $< 500$

$> 900$ and $< 1000$

Name ______________________________



# Tic-Tac-Toe

How to Play:

1. Solve the problems in the first row of a game.
2. Mark the gameboard with an X or O for the largest answer.
3. Continue to solve the problems in each row to try to get three in a row.

## Game 1

| X | O |
|---|---|
| 374 + 263 = ____ | 429 + 187 = ____ |
| 154 + 199 = ____ | 740 − 286 = ____ |
| 643 + 208 = ____ | 341 + 459 = ____ |
| 973 − 784 = ____ | 514 − 188 = ____ |
| 291 + 263 = ____ | 445 + 375 = ____ |

## Game 2

| X | O |
|---|---|
| 166 + 117 = ____ | 149 + 69 = ____ |
| 801 − 389 = ____ | 722 − 305 = ____ |
| 318 + 218 = ____ | 266 + 243 = ____ |
| 576 + 268 = ____ | 607 + 266 = ____ |
| 629 − 457 = ____ | 785 − 657 = ____ |

**Page 4**

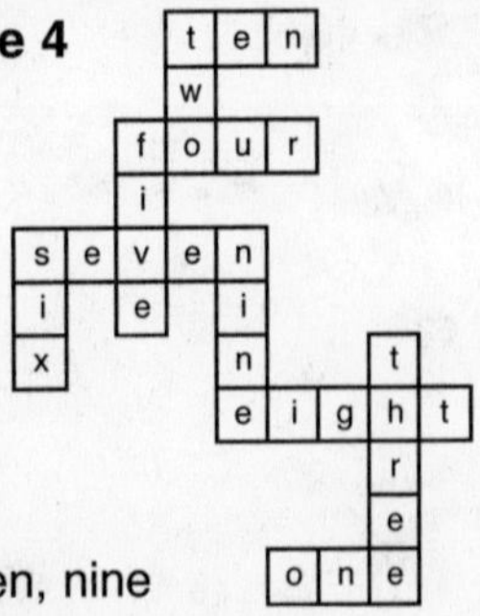

seven, nine

**Page 5**
Check that the child has drawn the correct number of petals on each flower. Bows with 4, 6, 8, and 10 should be colored yellow. Bows with 3, 5, 7, and 9 should be colored purple.

**Page 6**

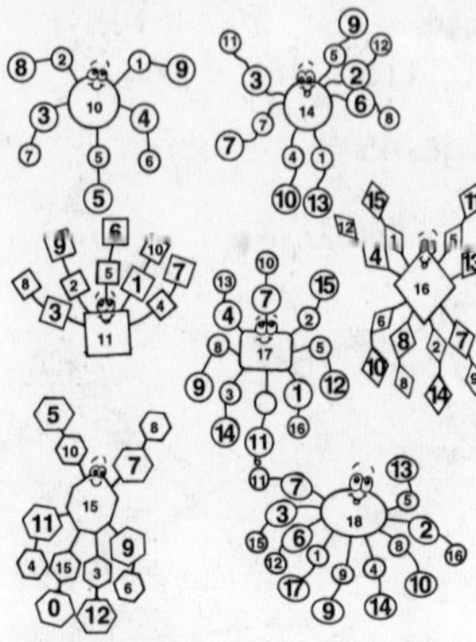

**Page 7**
A. 3, 2; B. 12, 5; C. 8, 6; D. 11, 7; E. 7, 5; F. 12, 3; G. 4, 1; H. 10, 8; I. 9, 4; J. 11, 5; Answers will vary.

**Page 8**
21, 93, 78, 46, 44, 78; PLEASE

50, 67, 46, 79, 83, 59, 25, 66; THANK YOU

59, 25, 66, 32, 78; YOU'RE

80, 78, 93, 18, 25, 35, 78; WELCOME

**Page 9**

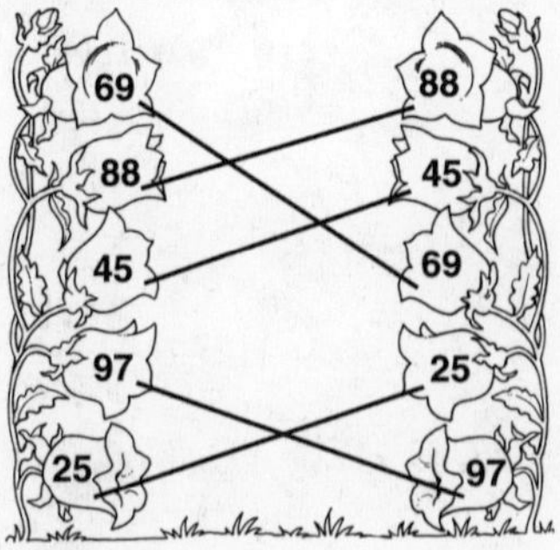


Answers will vary.

**Page 10**
38, 26, 97, 58, 67, 76, 79; 46, 84, 46, 89, 58, 48, 97; 58, 55, 65, 46, 40; THREE-FOURTHS, PACIFIC

**Page 11**
62, 33, 23; 30, 21, 14; 61, 22, 41; The bird with the difference of 30 should be colored red. The bird with the difference of 14 should be colored blue. The birds with the differences of 22 and 33 should be colored green.

**Page 12**

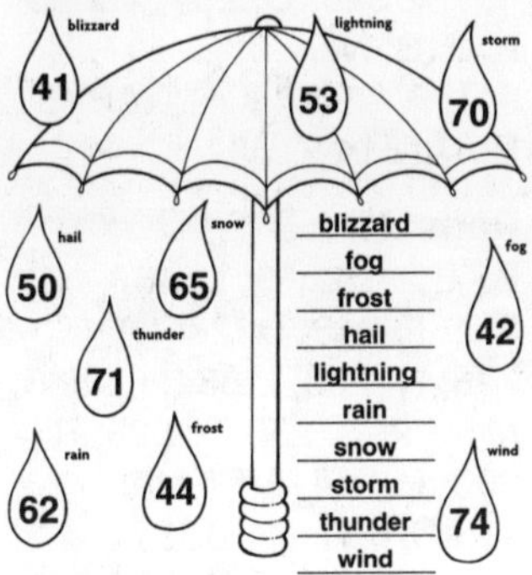


**Page 13**
54, 85, 43, 85; 43, 54, 67; 43, 67, 32; 32; Check child's coloring.

**Page 14**
10, 12, 16; 18, 14, 19; 15, 11, 17; Bowls with 11, 15, and 18 should be colored yellow. Bowls with 10, 14, and 17 should be colored pink. Bowls with 12, 16, and 18 should be colored brown.

**Page 15**

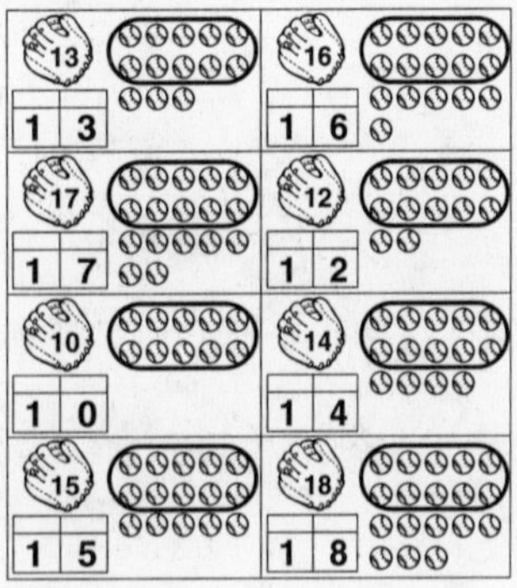


**Page 16**
A. 52, 93, 72, 93; B. 41, 62, 37, 37; C. 23, 50, 62, 62; D. 60, 32, 81, 60; E. 90, 44, 76, 44

**Page 17**

| | | | | |
|---|---|---|---|---|
| | 71 | 93 | 90 | 52 |
| 92 | 90 | 91 | 86 | 92 |
| 81 | 81 | 73 | 42 | 92 |
| 85 | 74 | 92 | 90 | 94 |
| 51 | 41 | 93 | 81 | |

**Page 18**
Beach: Route #1—13 + 48 + 32 + 54 = 147 miles; Route #2—13 + 48 + 88 + 39 = 188 miles

Mountains: Route #1—13 + 17 + 31 + 49 = 110 miles; Route #2—13 + 28 + 10 + 25 = 76 miles

**Page 19**
35: 3 tens 5 ones, 2 tens 15 ones; 47: 4 tens 7 ones, 3 tens 17 ones; 82: 8 tens 2 ones, 7 tens 12 ones; 94: 9 tens 4 ones, 8 tens 14 ones; 61: 6 tens 1 one, 5 tens 11 ones; 90: 9 tens 0 ones, 8 tens 10 ones

**Page 20**
Boldfaced numbers should be circled.

A. **48**, 89; B. 79, **46**; C. 36, **76**; D. **77**, 59; E. **48**, 14; F. 61, **68**; G. 14, **39**; Answers will vary.

**Page 21**
A. 19, 39, 37; 1, 3, 2; B. 8, 6, 9; 2, 1, 3; C. 28, 37, 14; 2, 3, 1; D. 29, 38, 37; 1, 3, 2; E. 29, 36, 48; 1, 2, 3; F. 18, 15, 19; 2, 1, 3

**Page 22**
65 – 27 = 38, 38 + 27 = 65; 77 – 38 = 39, 39 + 38 = 77; 24 – 15 = 9, 9 + 15 = 24; 32 – 13 = 19, 19 + 13 = 32; 83 – 49 = 34, 34 + 49 = 83; 50 – 19 = 31, 31 + 19 = 50; 46 – 29 = 17, 17 + 29 = 46; 62 – 15 = 47, 47 + 15 = 62

Answers will vary.

**Page 23**
U. 81; L. 5; N. 60; C. 46; O. 90; P. 38; H. 23; K. 63; S. 48; A. 14; G. 18; M. 71; R. 69; KANGAROO; KOALA; OPOSSUM; POUCH

**Page 24**
Check that the child has colored the appropriate spaces. A. 21; B. 9; C. 26; D. 8; E. 13; F. 17; G. 30; H. 7

**Page 25**
A. 28 + 25 = 53; B. 25 – 9 = 16; C. 28 – 13 = 15; D. 12 + 9 = 21; E. 12 – 9 = 3; F. 13 + 28 = 41; G. 9 + 25 + 12 = 46; 98 students

**Page 26**
saw: 34 + 27 + 5 = 66; wrench: 48 + 36 + 15 = 99; hammer: 43 + 15 + 27 = 85; pliers: 39 + 34 + 15 = 88; A. 27 + 15 = 42; B. 34 – 5 = 29, 48 – 15 = 33, 43 – 15 = 28; 39 – 15 = 24; 43 + 15 + 27 + 5 + 34 + 39 + 48 + 15 + 36 = 262

**Page 27**
A. 596, red; B. 995, blue; C. 877, blue; D. 569, blue; E. 662, red; F. 978, red; G. 968, red; H. 596, red; I. 899, blue; J. 497, blue

**Page 28**
2 hundreds 7 tens, 8 hundreds 4 tens, 9 hundreds 3 tens, 7 hundreds 1 ten; 5 hundreds 6 tens, 3 hundreds 2 tens, 4 hundreds 9 tens, 6 hundreds 5 tens; 570; 804

**Page 29**

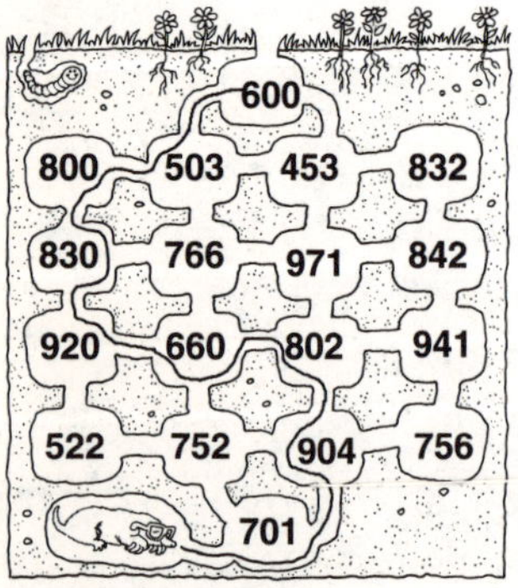


Problems will vary.

**Page 30**
A. $1.49 + $.50 + $.75 + $1.22 = $3.96; B. $1.72 + $.65 + $1.17 = $3.54; C. $1.86 + $1.84 + $.84 + $1.07 = $5.61; D. $1.53 + $1.90 + $1.22 + $.84 = $5.49; E. $1.86 + $.50 + $1.17 = $3.53; F. $1.49 + $.86 + $.75 = $3.10

**Page 31**
A. 123 + 406 + 406 = 935, orange; B. 209 + 81 + 147 + 181 + 72 = 690, green; C. 146 + 266 + 120 + 139 + 82 = 753, purple; D. 180 + 169 + 308 + 122 = 779, yellow; E. 154 + 154 + 188 + 93 + 82 + 170 = 841, red; F. 107 + 173 + 38 + 280 + 38 + 54 + 78 = 768, blue

**Page 32**
40 tens, 20 tens, 70 tens, 50 tens; 10 tens, 90 tens, 80 tens, 30 tens

**Page 33**

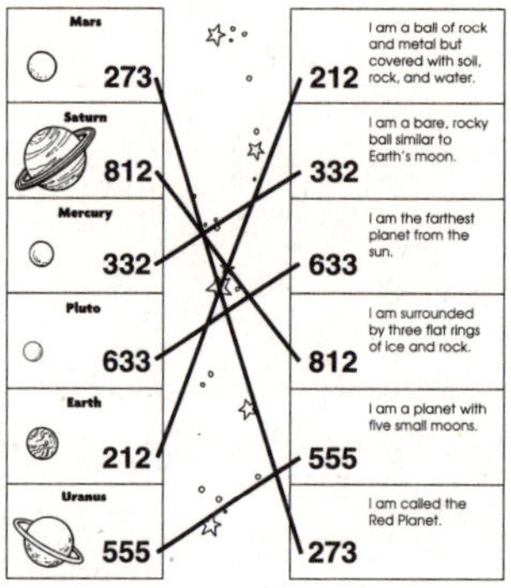


**Page 34**

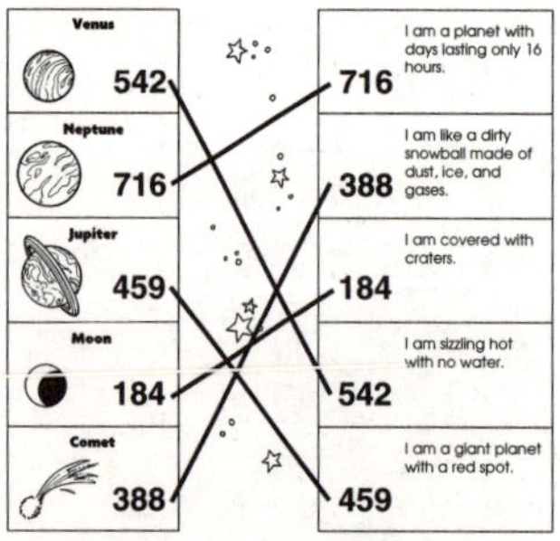


900, 800, 700, 600, 500, 400, 300, 200, 100, Subtract 100.; 900, 700, 500, 300, 100, Subtract 200.; 800, 600, 400, 200, Subtract 200.

**Page 35**

**Page 36**

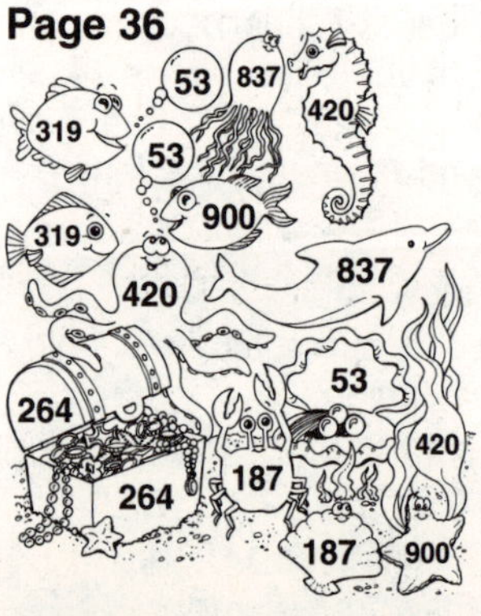


Check child's coloring.

**Page 37**

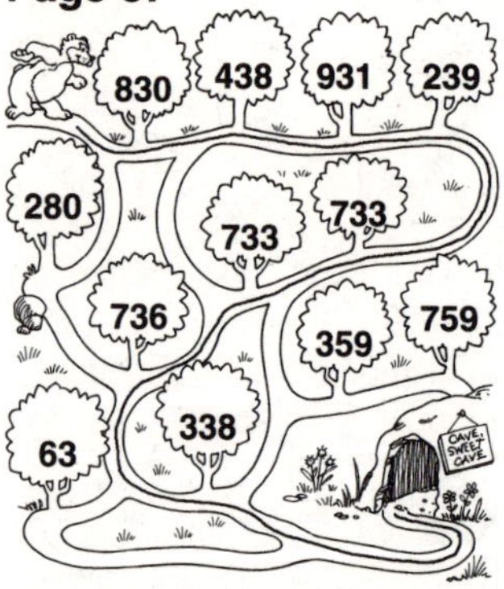


**Page 38**
A. 700 – 523 = 177; B. 300 – 156 = 144; C. 248 + 176 = 424, 600 – 424 = 176; D. 189 + 96 = 285, 400 – 285 = 115; E. 398 + 275 = 673, 900 – 673 = 227

**Page 39**
A. 168 – 159 = 9; B. 427 + 289 = 716; C. 507 – 278 = 229; D. 319 + 299 = 618; E. 826 – 697 = 129; F. 258 + 273 = 531

**Page 40**
T. 500; O. 903; L. 285; P. 846; A. 535; W. 951; I. 870; P. 528; L. 979; I. 207; R. 821; I. 564; O. 254; A. 853; N. 273; N. 869; R. 517; H. 811; A. 894; LION, TAPIR, PIRANHA, OWL

**Page 41**
B. 773; E. 569; L. 467; H. 374; F. 248; D. 385; A. 796; N. 288; I. 834; O. 883; M. 689; C. 259; T. 896; R. 800; P. 704; FIREMAN, TEACHER, DOCTOR, LIBRARIAN, POLICEMAN

**Page 42**
sandals $2.10 + swimsuits $6.89 + sand toys $1.23 + swim ring $1.46 = $11.68

mittens $.77 + coat $7.14 + hat $1.23 + skis $3.74 = $12.88

$12.88 – $11.68 = $1.20

**Page 43**

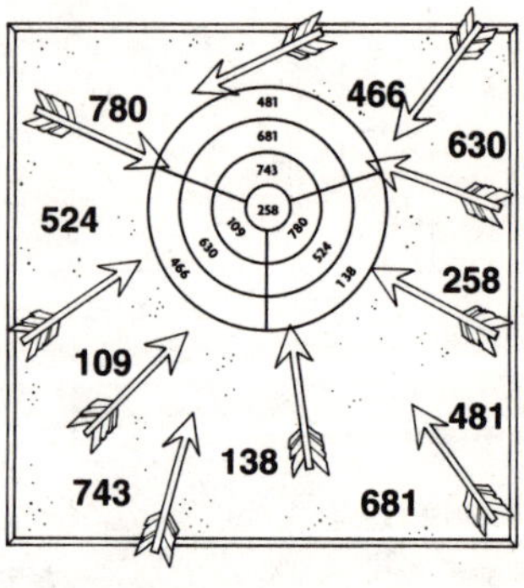


Answers will vary.

**Page 44**
427 + 282 = 709, 636 – 550 = 86; 963 – 189 = 774, 148 + 370 = 518, 550 + 370 = 920, 804 – 636 = 168; 189 + 751 = 940, 579 – 282 = 297, 963 – 148 = 815, 415 + 189 = 604

**Page 45**

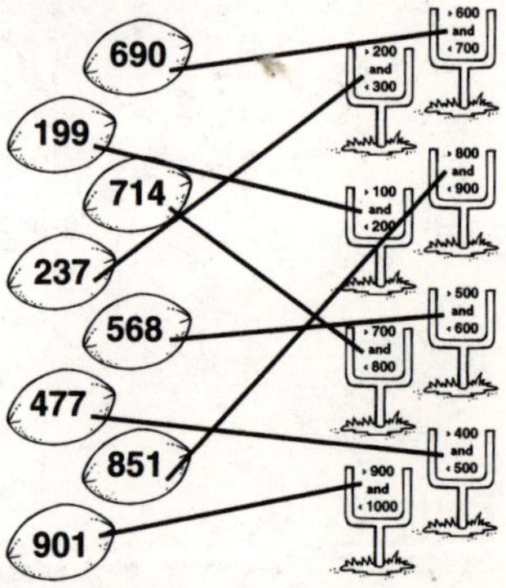


**Page 46**
Game 1: 637, 616; 353, 454; 851, 800; 189, 326; 554, 820

Game 2: 283, 218; 412, 417; 536, 509; 844, 873; 172, 128